GUIDE TO CHINA

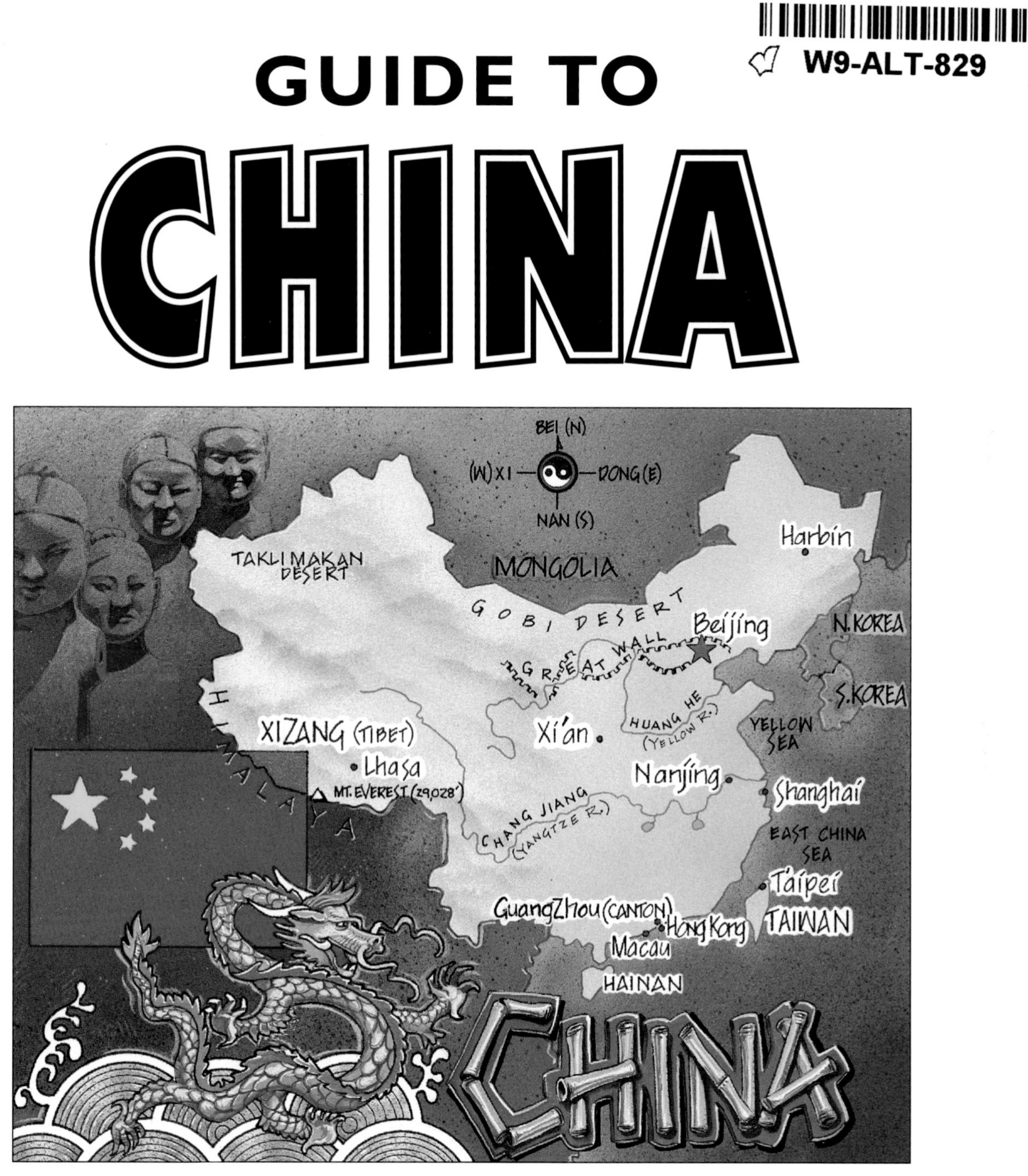

MIKE MARCH

Highlights for Children

Contents

On the cover: Tourists walk along the Great Wall of China, a 3,700-mile (5,920-kilometer) wall built more than 2,000 years ago.

The publisher is grateful for the assistance of Ethan M. Jennings, a graduate student in the International Studies program at the University of California, Berkeley, for reviewing this book. Mr. Jennings has studied in Chinese-language classes at Suzhou University, Suzhou, China, and has also attended universities in Russia and the Czech Republic.

Published by Highlights for Children

P.O. Box 18201
Columbus, Ohio 43218-0201
For information on *Top Secret Adventures,* visit www.tsadventures.com or call 1-800-962-3661.

15 14 HPS
ISBN 978-0-87534-918-3

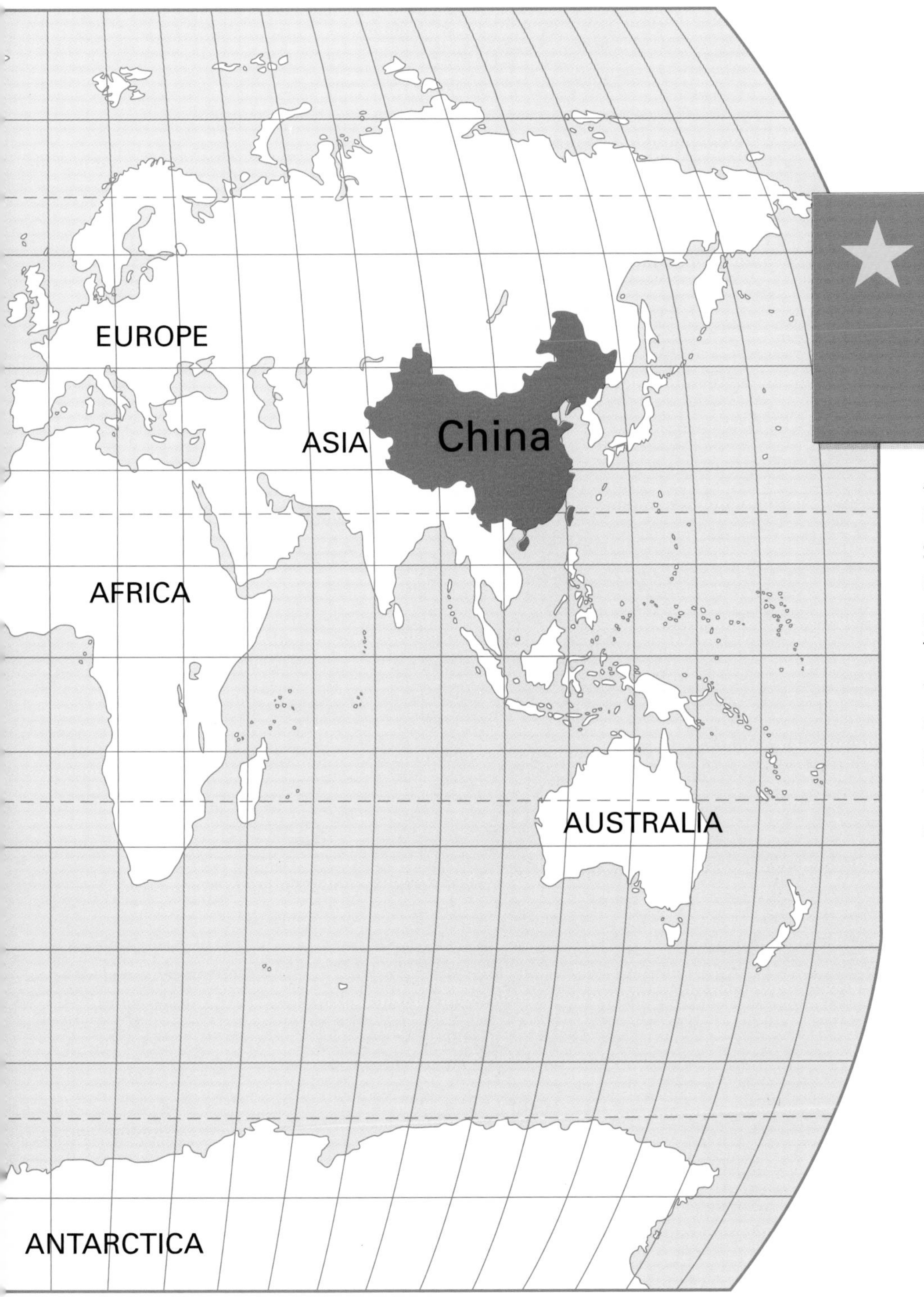

△ **China's flag** The red flag with gold stars was chosen by China's Communist government in 1949. The biggest star on the flag represents the Communist Party. China's official name is the People's Republic of China.

CHINA AT A GLANCE

Area 3,705,405 square miles (9,596,960 square kilometers)
Population 1,343,239,923
Capital Beijing (Peking), population 12,214,000
Other big cities Shanghai (population 16,575,000), Chongqing (9,401,000)
Highest mountain Zhumulangma Feng (Mt. Everest), 29,035 feet (8,850 meters)
Longest river Chang Jiang (Yangtze), 3,960 miles (6,380 kilometers)
Largest lake Qinghai, 1,660 square miles (4,100 square kilometers)
Official language Putonghua, or Mandarin Chinese

▽ **Chinese stamps** China's natural wonders as well as cultural artifacts are featured on stamps.

▷ **Chinese money** China's currency is the *yuan* or *renminbi*. There are ten *jiao* to one yuan.

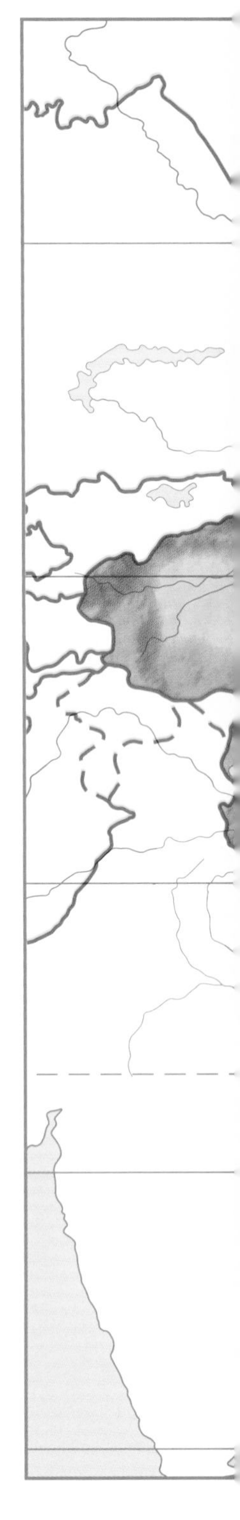

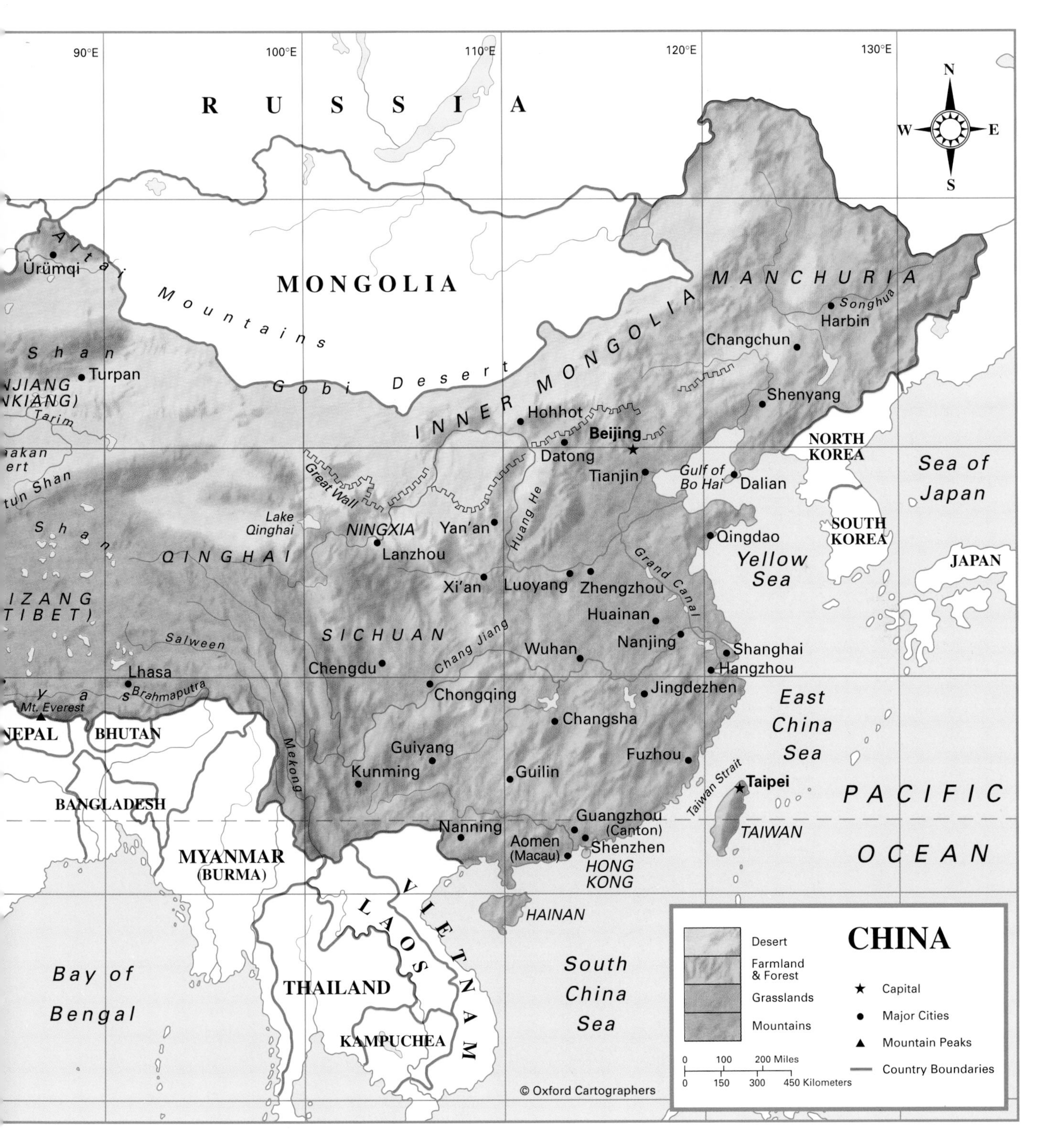
90°E
100°E
110°E
120°E
130°E
N
W
E
S
RUSSIA
MONGOLIA
Altai Mountains
Ürümqi
Gobi Desert
MANCHURIA
INNER MONGOLIA
Songhua
Harbin
Changchun
Shenyang
Turpan
Tarim
Hohhot
Beijing
Datong
Tianjin
NORTH KOREA
Gulf of Bo Hai
Dalian
Sea of Japan
Great Wall
Huang He
Lake Qinghai
NINGXIA
Yan'an
Lanzhou
QINGHAI
Qingdao
SOUTH KOREA
Yellow Sea
JAPAN
Grand Canal
Xi'an
Luoyang
Zhengzhou
Huainan
SICHUAN
Nanjing
Salween
Chang Jiang
Wuhan
Shanghai
Chengdu
Hangzhou
Lhasa
Brahmaputra
Chongqing
Jingdezhen
Mt. Everest
East China Sea
Changsha
NEPAL
BHUTAN
Mekong
Guiyang
Fuzhou
Kunming
Guilin
Taiwan Strait
Taipei
PACIFIC OCEAN
BANGLADESH
Guangzhou (Canton)
TAIWAN
Nanning
Aomen (Macau)
Shenzhen
HONG KONG
MYANMAR (BURMA)
VIETNAM
LAOS
HAINAN
Bay of Bengal
THAILAND
KAMPUCHEA
South China Sea
CHINA
Desert
Farmland & Forest
Grasslands
Mountains
Capital
Major Cities
Mountain Peaks
Country Boundaries
0 100 200 Miles
0 150 300 450 Kilometers
© Oxford Cartographers

ASIA'S GIANT

China is one of the largest countries on Earth. It fills most of the eastern part of the continent of Asia. China is a land of snowcapped mountains, sandy deserts, grassy plains, and thousands of rivers and lakes. A long coastline dotted with tiny islands forms its eastern border. Here, two of the world's great rivers, the Chang Jiang (*jiang* means river) and the Huang He, flow into the sea.

South of the Chang Jiang, the weather is warm all year round, with plenty of rain. In the north, the winters are bitterly cold. While farmers in the south are planting rice, people in the north are still clearing snow from the streets. In dry areas, monsoon rains start in late spring and end in the fall. Floods and typhoons present other dangers.

More than a billion people live in China. More than a quarter of them are farmers. They live in the southern and eastern parts of the country. Many people also live in the cities. China is home to one of the world's oldest civilizations. The Chinese people invented many things, including the printing process, paper, gunpowder, the compass, porcelain, and silk.

Ninety-one percent of the people who live in this huge country are of Chinese ancestry. The rest come from more than fifty ethnic groups. Some, like the people of Tibet and Mongolia, have their own language. The way people speak Chinese varies greatly across the country. People from Guangzhou in the south and people from Beijing in the north find it difficult to understand each other. Traveling around China by train is a good way to meet the people. You will always be greeted with a smile, so smile back. For longer journeys, airplanes fly between most of the big cities.

▷ **Rice fields near Guilin, southern China** Farmers plant seeds in flooded fields called paddies. Most of China's rice grows south of the Chang Jiang.

▷ **Chinese peasants at work on a farm**
For 7,000 years Chinese people have been farmers. But, even today, only one-tenth of the land in China is good for growing crops.

▽ **A Chinese craftworker painting a porcelain vase**
Porcelain is made from a clay called *kaolin*, which is baked in an oven. Because this process was invented here, this pottery and other fine dishes are often called china.

The Northern Capital

China's capital is the famous ancient city of Beijing. The name means "northern capital." In English, the old name of the capital was Peking. When Beijing was first built 3,000 years ago, it was a little town called Ji. Today it is a bustling city. More than 12 million people live here. Many of them use bicycles to get around in the city.

▽ **Peking Roast Duck** Known the world over, Peking Duck is an example of Beijing-style cooking. The duck skin is brushed with molasses so it turns dark.

In the center of Beijing is the huge Tiananmen Square. When the square was first built hundreds of years ago, it was much smaller. But in the 1950s, on the instructions of China's leader Mao Zedong, builders knocked down old buildings and walls nearby. They made the square larger and widened the streets around it.

Mao was China's first Communist head of state. He died in 1976 and his tomb was built on the square. Nearby is the Great Hall of the People, where the present People's Congress meets. One of its many rooms is a banquet hall big enough for 5,000 people.

The square takes its name from the high wooden building on its north side — Tiananmen, which means "Gate of Heavenly Peace." At one time, only the emperor was allowed to use Tiananmen's middle entrance.

To get around the city, you can rent a bicycle and join the people on the roads. You can also go by bus or taxi or take the subway. Shopping in Beijing is easiest at the large department stores. Here, you will find all kinds of traditional goods, including jade ornaments, silk shirts, china tea sets, and paper kites. Eating out is fun, too. Peking Roast Duck is a local dish that is known all over the world. But the best place to try it is here in Beijing. The Beijing Opera is just as famous. People enjoy this age-old form of musical drama for its bright colors and beautiful costumes, as well as for its music.

◁ **Tiananmen Square seen from the "Gate of Heavenly Peace"** A stream crossed by seven bridges separates the gate from the square. The building in the center is Mao Zedong's tomb.

▽ **Bicyclists on Chang'an Boulevard** Riding a bicycle is easy in Beijing because there are few hills. But at times, the streets are so crowded with bicycles and cars that there are traffic jams.

WALLS AND EMPERORS

A cobblestone road from Tiananmen leads to the Imperial Palace. For 500 years this was the home of China's emperors. The royal palaces and their land were a separate city inside Beijing. They stood on an island, cut off from the main city by a wide moat and high walls. To the ordinary people, this was the Forbidden City. They dared not enter.

▽ **The Hall of Prayer for Good Harvests in the Garden of the Temple of Heaven**
This magnificent building was built without using any nails.

The biggest and finest of the palaces is the Hall of Supreme Harmony. The emperors were crowned here. People would pay their respects by bowing nine times to the ringing of a gong.

Once a year, the emperor led a parade of people, chariots, and elephants from the Forbidden City to the Temple of Heaven. There, he would pray for a good harvest. The ordinary people were not allowed to see the emperor. They had to hide themselves indoors whenever he passed.

China's emperors always feared attacks by the warlike peoples who lived on their northern borders. Over hundreds of years, the Chinese built a colossal defensive wall across the north of the country. The Great Wall of China is approximately 3,700 miles (5,920 kilometers) long. You can visit one of the best-preserved sections of the wall at Badaling, about 50 miles (80 kilometers) from Beijing. From here, the guards from the beacon towers could send smoke signals to the capital to warn of approaching danger.

Nearby are the tombs of the Ming emperors who built much of China's Great Wall and the Forbidden City. The path to the tombs, called the "Spirit Way," is guarded by huge stone statues of warriors and animals. If you come here, try making a wish and then throwing a small stone. It is said that if the stone lands on an animal's back, your wish will come true!

◁ **The Forbidden City seen from Coal Hill** The hill was built from the dirt that was dug out to make the Forbidden City's moat. All the buildings face south.

▽ **The Great Wall of China** The wall winds its way up mountains, down valleys, over grassland, and across desert.

Cities and Canals

For more than 300 years China's capital city was Hangzhou, a port on the East China Sea. To travel here by train from Beijing takes around twenty-four hours.

The famous Italian explorer Marco Polo traveled to Hangzhou in the 13th century. It was then called "the Heavenly City," and he described it as the most beautiful he had ever seen. China was one of the most advanced countries in the world. Its people were the first to use paper money. They also used a bead frame, called an abacus, to calculate mathematics answers. It is still used today.

You can visit Hangzhou's beautiful old temples and pagodas. Many of these have been restored or rebuilt. Next to the town's old quarter is the lovely Xi Hu, or West Lake. There are four islands in the lake, each with a pagoda or pavilion. The lake is surrounded by hills on three sides.

▽ **Shanghai skyline** The Oriental Pearl TV Tower, far left, stands out among the many skyscrapers that make up the Shanghai skyline.

▽ **Chinese acrobats** The world-famous Shanghai acrobatic team puts on a thrilling show. They perform most nights of the week.

▷ **China's Grand Canal** The Chinese invented the canal lock, so that ships can move between different water levels.

Hangzhou lies at the southern end of the Grand Canal. This famous waterway links the city with Beijing, far to the north. For many centuries, rice grown in the south was loaded onto barges and sailing ships called *junks*. The rice was shipped northward along the canal to feed the emperor and his armies. The canal was dug by many millions of men and women. It took nearly 2,000 years to build the great waterway. Today, some of the northern part is filled with mud. But, farther south, heavy goods, such as coal and fruit and vegetables, still move by canal.

Shanghai is northeast of Hangzhou. With its sixteen million people, Shanghai is the biggest and busiest city in China. You see all kinds of factories here and lots of ships in the country's biggest harbor. Behind the main avenues and shops, there are crowded narrow streets and colorful markets.

UP THE CHANG JIANG

One of the best hotels in China is the Jingling Hotel in the center of the city of Nanjing. This skyscraper stands 37 stories high. There is a revolving restaurant at the top. From here, you can enjoy a meal and have a fine view of the surrounding city.

The body of Sun Yat-sen, the "father of modern China," is buried in the hills to the east. Sun was elected president in 1911. You can visit his huge blue-and-white tomb, set in its own grounds. Nearby is the ancient tomb of the Hongwu emperor, who made Nanjing his capital.

△ **Jialing Jiang, Chongqing** The Old Town on the hillside overlooks the river. Around the bend, the Jialing meets the Chang Jiang.

To the northwest, one of the longest bridges in China carries buses, cars, trucks, and trains across the mighty Chang Jiang, the river once known as the Yangtze. The bridge links the north and the south of the country. A second bridge, crosses the Chang Jiang at Wuhan, farther upstream. From this city you can board a riverboat for a five-day voyage up the Chang Jiang. During your journey you will see steamships, hydrofoils, and traditional sailing junks on the river.

The wide channel of the Chang Jiang at Wuhan is surrounded by dikes to prevent flooding. Farther upstream the river narrows as it cuts its way through the Three Gorges. This part of the river is an astonishing sight. The water rushes between the sheer cliffs and mountains on the riverbanks. The government is building one of the world's largest dams to generate electricity and make it easier for ships to pass through the gorges. Eventually, you leave the riverboat at Chongqing. This industrial town is in Sichuan province. Here, you can enjoy the favorite local dish of skewered pork cooked in spicy oil.

◁ **Crowds waiting to board the riverboat at Badong** Most boats can go only as far west as Chongqing. The Chang is the third-longest river in the world.

▷ **Bridge over the Chang Jiang at Nanjing** The huge bridge was built between 1960 and 1968. The railroad bridge is more than four miles (6.4 kilometers) long. The road bridge stretches for one and a half miles (2.4 kilometers).

Southern Frontiers

The city of Kunming in southwestern China is the capital of Yunnan province. It is called the "city of eternal spring." Camellias, marigolds, rhododendrons, or other flowers are always in bloom. Many different peoples have their homes in Kunming. Stroll along the shaded avenues or through the narrow alleys crowded with bicycles and pony carts. You will often see people proudly wearing their national costumes. You may even come across sword-swallowers or other exciting street performers.

▽ **Water buffalo plowing flooded rice fields** At harvest time, the buffalo trample on the crop to separate the grain.

▽ **Zhu Jiang, in the middle of Guangzhou** From the dock, the tourist ferry goes downriver, passing sailing junks, flat-bottomed sampans, freighters, naval gunboats, and sometimes huge oil tankers.

◁ **Traditional wooden houses in Kunming** The city, in central Yunnan, has mild weather all year round. Northern Yunnan, near the mountains of Tibet, is chilly. The southern part of the province has a tropical rain forest.

Guangzhou is southern China's biggest city and seaport. It used to be known as Canton. The city lies on the Zhu River, which flows into the South China Sea. Rice paddies around the city are irrigated by the waters of the Zhu. Farmers plant and harvest three rice crops a year. Tea and tobacco are also grown here, as well as pineapples, bananas, mandarin oranges, and sugarcane. The many factories in Guangzhou build buses, ships, machinery, and electronic goods.

The beautiful Temple of Six Banyan Trees is in the old part of the city. It was built more than 1,400 years ago. The temple has been restored many times. The banyan trees once stood in the courtyard, but they are long gone. Overlooking the temple is the huge Flower Pagoda. By the north bank of the Zhu, Shamian Island has old European-style houses. These were built by the British and French, who once lived here.

Cantonese food, such as sweet and sour pork, stuffed dumplings, spring rolls, and meat in rice pastry pouches, is popular all over the world. Qingping market sells dried starfish, deer antlers, and tree bark. All are used by cooks here.

The China Coast

Hainan Island is a tropical paradise in the South China Sea. Boats going to the island leave Guangzhou from the south side of the Zhu River. When you get there, you can relax on unspoiled, white sandy beaches and dine on coconuts. Most of China's rubber comes from trees grown on Hainan Island. The rare Hainan deer lives here.

From Guangzhou, you can also take a hovercraft to the much smaller island of Hong Kong, near the mouth of the Zhu. For more than a hundred years, Hong Kong and its neighboring territories belonged to Great Britain. But there are many more Chinese people here than British. This land was given back to China in 1997. Hong Kong has one of the finest natural harbors in the world, and one of the busiest. There are skyscrapers, international banks, modern factories, and warehouses. But overcrowding is a major problem. Many poor people live on boats or in rundown shacks.

Facing Hong Kong is Aomen, once governed by the Portuguese. The towering ruins of the burned-out church of São Paulo is a famous local landmark.

About 100 miles (160 kilometers) out to sea lies the rocky island of Taiwan. To the government in Beijing, Taiwan is a province of China. To the people of the island, it is the rightful home of the Chinese government. When the Communists came to power in 1949, their rivals, the Nationalists, fled to Taiwan. They set up their own government in the capital city, Taipei. Today, Taiwan is a big producer of electronic goods, such as cameras, televisions, and computers, as well as machinery.

◁ **A street in Taipei, Taiwan's capital** Most tourists to Taipei visit the National Palace Museum with its treasures of ancient China.

◁ **Aberdeen Harbor, Hong Kong** Thousands of people live on sampans and junks in the port, overlooked by modern skyscrapers.

▽ **Lantern Festival, Hong Kong** The Chinese New Year is followed by the Lantern Festival. All over China, people hang up beautiful lanterns, bought from shops like this, and eat sweet balls of rice filled with nuts.

The "Roof of the World"

You can take an airplane from Guangzhou to Lhasa. This is the capital of the beautiful mountain region that we call Tibet. Tibetan people call it Bodjul. In Chinese, it is called Xizang. The Tibetan plateau is so high and wide that it is called the "roof of the world." This is a land of mountains, deserts, and high plains. Fewer people live here than in any other region of China.

Lhasa is an ancient and lovely city. The magnificent Potala Palace stands on the site of a palace built by the great Tibetan king Songsten Gampo in the seventh century A.D. The building that you see today was once the home of the Dalai Lama, Tibet's religious leader. The Dalai Lama now lives in exile in India. The Tibetan religion came from Buddhism. This religion arrived in China from India in the third century A.D. You can easily spot Tibetan monks by their long red robes and shaven heads.

Most people here survive by raising long-haired yaks, goats, sheep, and horses. Barley is the traditional crop. In the warmer valleys farmers also grow oats, maize, and sweet potatoes.

▷ **Tibetan girl** She belongs to the Khampa people of eastern Tibet. Traditionally, they braid their hair with red thread. The men often carry swords and daggers.

The deserts and grasslands of Tibet, where little grows, are rich in minerals. Coal, uranium, and oil have been taken from the earth. Salt is collected from the lakes. High winds sweep the plateau on its northern rim. The winds whip up snowstorms in winter and sandstorms at other times of the year. Here, in the world's second-largest nature reserve, the snow leopard lives undisturbed. Mount Everest, or Zhumulangma Feng as the local people call it, rises above Tibet's border with Nepal. At 29,035 feet (8,850 meters), it is the world's highest peak.

◁ **Potala Palace** The fine palace rises thirteen stories and has 1,000 rooms. It was built in the seventeenth century. It has been used as a palace, a fortress, a monastery, and as a prison.

▷ **Yaks in the Tibetan hills** The shaggy-coated oxen are kept for their milk, meat, and skins. Tibetans like drinking tea flavored with yak's butter. Yaks can also pull a cart and carry a heavy load, or they can be ridden. Many still roam wild.

TRADE AND CONQUEST

Kashgar is the westernmost town in China. It lies on an oasis at the edge of the Taklimakan Desert. Long ago, traders from Arabia and India passed this way with their camel caravans. They were traveling toward the cities of northern China to buy silk. The long and hard route they followed across Asia became known as the Silk Road.

Silk comes from the silkworm. It is really the cocoon of this special kind of caterpillar. In the ancient world, silk was very valuable. For a long time, only the Chinese knew the secret of how to make it. Merchants carried glass, jewelry, spices, perfumes, and other precious goods along the Silk Road to China. They traded them for Chinese silk.

Islam, a religion that started in Arabia, was also brought to China by the merchants. Many people in Kashgar and in northwestern China follow Islam and worship in a mosque. They are mostly Uigurs, who are distant cousins of the Turkish people.

Farther east, at the edge of the Gobi Desert, lie the grasslands of Inner Mongolia. Traditionally, the Mongols raised horses and herded sheep. They lived in huts made of animal hide, called *yurts*. These could be taken down and moved. You can watch a display of Mongolian horseback riding in the town of Hohhot. You can even arrange to spend a night sleeping out in a yurt.

The Mongols once ruled all of China, creating the Yuan dynasty. Kublai Khan, grandson of the great Mongol leader Genghis Khan, made Beijing his capital city in 1271. But in 1368 the empire fell. The Mongols went back to their former home on the other side of the Great Wall.

△ **A Mongolian summer fair** People set up their yurts on the grasslands and play traditional sports. They race horses, practice archery, wrestle, and sometimes race camels.

▷ **Heavenly Lake (Tianchi), near the oasis city of Ürümqi** The lake lies in the middle of mountains that are surrounded by desert.

◁ **Idh Kah Mosque, Kashgar**
The mosque holds 8,000 people. Its tall, thin towers are called minarets. From here, the Islamic priest calls Muslims to prayer. The mosque is nearly 200 years old.

The Golden Age

More than a thousand years ago, Xi'an was China's capital. At that time it may have been the greatest city in the world. It was full of beautiful palaces, temples, and pagodas. The Silk Road started in Xi'an. For hundreds of years this route brought merchants to China from as far away as Europe. Art and learning were encouraged by leaders in the city. The first printed book was published here.

You can walk around the top of the old city walls. In fact, the walls are so wide that two chariots could pass each other with plenty of room to spare.

In a suburb of Xi'an lie the dugout ruins of a village that is 6,000 years old. You can see the remains of the villagers' houses. You will find stone axes and fishhooks that were their tools, ovens where they baked pottery, and their graves.

▽ **The terra-cotta army** More than 7,000 clay figures have been discovered at the tomb of China's first emperor. Many of them were broken and had to be carefully pieced together.

▽ **The Great Wild Goose Pagoda, Xi'an** The building is made of brick. It was built during China's "golden age."

The first emperor to rule all of China is buried near Xi'an. He was called Qin Shi Huangdi. For 2,000 years, a huge army of warriors, chariots, and horses has stood guard over his tomb. Of course, this is not a real army. The soldiers are made of a red clay, called terra-cotta. They are life size and once carried real swords and spears.

Xi'an lies in the middle of rich farming land. Here, a thick layer of yellow-brown dust has built up over millions of years. The dust covers the earth and colors the rivers. The mightiest of these rivers is the Huang He. The name means "yellow river" in Chinese. Over the centuries, the Huang He has changed course many times and washed away many farms and villages in its floods. Dams and dikes have been built to help control the great river.

▽ **Early morning exercises on the banks of the Huang He** Groups of people enjoy *taijiquan*, or *tai chi*. This popular traditional form of exercise helps keep them fit.

Manchuria

Winter comes early to Heilongjiang province, in northeastern China. Along the border with Russia, snow lies on the ground for nine months of the year. People buy milk in frozen bricks of ice. The main city here is Harbin. One hundred years ago it was a small fishing village. Then the Russians built the Trans-Siberian Railroad. It passed through the province, and Harbin grew rapidly. Today it is a city of more than five million people.

January is a good time to visit Harbin, but only if you can stand the fierce cold and the biting winds. This is the time of year when the people who live here celebrate the International Ice and Snow Festival. All over the city, strange but beautiful lanterns made of ice are hung from the houses. And fantastic sculptures of temples, boats, and animals are molded in ice. They are lit up with colored lights and displayed in public parks.

▷ **Workers outside a steel plant** The city of Anshan, the "steel capital of China," is in Liaoning province.

The provinces of northeastern China were once called Manchuria. The Manchus were a people descended from the Mongols. They ruled China for nearly 300 years. But in 1911, China became free. The last Manchu emperor, Puyi, was forced to give up the crown. He was only eight years old at the time. In the 1930s, the Japanese invaded Manchuria. They made Changchun their capital and crowned Puyi emperor. Today, the palace where he lived is a museum.

Farther south, the big city of Shenyang was the stronghold of the early Manchu emperors. You can visit their great palaces and their tombs. Today, the city is the most important center for trade, industry, and culture in northeast China. From Shenyang, you can fly back to Beijing for one last look at China's capital before you leave for home.

◁ **Statue of Mao Zedong in Shenyang** The huge statue stands on Zhongshan Square, in the center of the city. The Communists, led by Mao, captured Shenyang in 1949. It has now grown into a big industrial city.

▷ **A Chinese steam locomotive** Steam trains still run in China, but they are being replaced by electric trains. Shenyang has the biggest steam engine museum in China.

CHINA FACTS AND FIGURES

People
More than nine-tenths of China's people are Han or ethnic Chinese. There are also more than fifty other ethnic groups living in China. The largest of the minority peoples are the Zhuang, who number about sixteen million.

Trade and Industry
China has rich mineral resources. More coal, iron ore, and tin are produced in China than in any other country in the world. Oil and gas are also plentiful. Most of the coal is found in northern China. Coal is used to create much of China's electricity. There are also hydroelectric plants in the south, as well as nuclear power stations.

China's exports include iron, steel, electrical machinery, and other machinery, including data processing equiptment The United States, Hong Kong, and Japan are China's top export partners.

In recent years, both European and American firms have been encouraged to build factories in China. Tourism is a growing industry, with more than 50 million foreign visitors a year.

△ **Lotus fields in southern China** The Chinese have always loved the lotus flower. They use it to make medicine. To Buddhists, it represents life, peace of mind, and justice.

Farming
Only one-tenth of China's land can be used for agriculture. Yet, two out of three Chinese work on the land. Rice is the main crop. China is one of the world's leading producers of rice, wheat, potatoes, peanuts, tea, barley, apples, cotton, oilseed, pork, and fish. Large areas of grazing land are found in the outer regions of China. Sheep, goats, cattle, and water buffalo are kept for their milk, meat, and hides. Wool and silk are also important products. Pigs, ducks, and chickens are raised in country regions.

Fishing
About two-thirds of China's fish are caught in the sea. The catch is higher in the south where the waters are much warmer. Seaweed and shellfish are taken from the shallow coastal waters. Freshwater fish are caught in the delta regions near the mouths of the Chang Jiang and Zhu rivers. Some lakes have also been stocked with fish, and species such as carp are bred on fish farms.

Food
Chinese dishes and styles of cooking vary from region to region.
Beijing style: Peking Roast Duck. Its juicy meat and crispy skin are served with green onions, paper-thin pancakes, and plum sauce.
Cantonese style: Popular foods include steamed dumplings filled with shrimp, deep-fried spring rolls, and steamed white rice.
Shanghai style: Near the sea, Shanghai is noted for its seafood, such as crabs, oysters, fish, and seaweed.
Szechuan style: This cuisine is known for its spicy dishes, such as Kung Pao Chicken.

Schools

Children can attend nursery school from the age of three. At six, they enter primary school, where they spend the next six years. They study math, Chinese language, a foreign language, history, geography, science, music, and art. All children must then attend secondary school. After three years, they can go to a special teacher-training, technical, or agricultural college or stay at school for another three years to study more general topics.

△ **A farmer's house in eastern China**
Traditional scrolls with Chinese writing hang from the wall. Bowls with chopsticks stand on the table.

Literature

More than 2,000 years ago, Chinese scholars wrote their history. The 7th to 13th centuries were the "golden age" of Chinese poetry. The first Chinese novels appeared in the 14th century. One of the best-known of these is *Water Margin* by Shi Naian. Famous Chinese writers of the 20th century include Lu Xun, Lao She, and Mao Dun. Their novels describe China in the 1920s and 1930s. During the 1980s, Ah Cheng became famous for his novel *Chess King*.

The Media

China has about 2,000 daily and weekly newspapers. The best-known national daily newspaper is the *Renmin Ribao* (People's Daily). The *China Daily* is published in English. There are also more than 2,000 magazines.

Hundreds of television and radio stations serve the country. Some of these broadcast programs in Mandarin Chinese across the whole of China. Programs in Chinese dialects, and sometimes in other languages, are produced for showing throughout the appropriate provinces.

Drama

Chinese theater began in the 12th century. It grew out of a tradition begun by singing Buddhist monks. Chinese opera developed as a popular form of drama. Most opera in China is in the Beijing style. The actors wear colorful costumes, and some wear masks. They sing, often in high-pitched voices, to the music of cymbals, lutes, and drums.

"Shadow play" puppet theater has been popular for 2,000 years. The puppets are worked by puppeteers behind a silk screen.

Art

Calligraphy is the ancient art of painting characters from the written Chinese language. The same tools are used as in Chinese picture painting—ink, a brush, and white paper.

Chinese potters have produced beautiful cups, bowls, and vases. By the 1300s, China was exporting porcelain vases to Europe. People carve bowls, bracelets, and other objects from the hard green stone called jade. An ancient Chinese craft is the use of lacquer, a rich varnish, to decorate boxes, fans, and furniture.

CHINA FACTS AND FIGURES

Religion
The most important religions are Daoism, Confucianism, and Buddhism. Daoism is based on the teachings of Lao zi, who lived 2,500 years ago. He thought that things are made up of two opposites, called Yin and Yang, which join to form a whole. Confucianism is named after Confucius, a famous Chinese philosopher who was born in 551 B.C. He taught that people should live in peace and respect each other. Buddhism, which came from India, teaches how to achieve peace of mind.

△ **Giant Panda** Most Pandas live in the bamboo forests of Sichuan. The Panda is a symbol of good luck to the Chinese people.

Sports
China's national sport is table tennis. People also enjoy swimming, soccer, badminton, and volleyball. Martial arts go back more than 2,000 years. Gongfu (or kungfu), belongs to this popular tradition. Opponents strike each other with their hands and feet. Taijiquan is a slow-motion form of exercise.

Festivals
China's many traditional festivals have no fixed dates. A few of them are listed here.

Spring Festival (Lunar New Year). People set off firecrackers and dance down the streets wearing dragon and lion masks.
Qingming Festival In spring, people offer food and drink to their ancestors, and they burn paper models in their honor.
Moon Festival It celebrates Mid-Fall Day, when the moon is full, and symbolizes unity of the family.

Plants
There are more than 2,800 kinds of trees in China. They range from fir and pine in the northeast to bamboo, farther south, and mangroves on the tropical south coast. Maple, birch, and ash trees also grow in the northeast. So does ginseng, a plant with red berries that is used as a medicine. The peony, chrysanthemum, lotus flower, and peach tree are important to the Chinese.

Animals
China has a huge variety of wildlife, including rare animals. The northeastern forests are home to the Amur leopard and Siberian tiger. Monkeys, tigers, elephants, leopards, and muntjac deer live in the tropical rain forests farther south. Wild camels, bears, foxes, and wolves inhabit grassland and deserts. The Chinese alligator lives only in the Chang Jiang. The rare Asiatic onager lives on China's border with Nepal. Giant pandas live in protected forests. Birds include one of the smallest birds in the world, the Pekin robin.

HISTORY

People have lived in China for more than a million years. About 8,000 years ago the first farming villages grew up around the Huang He. By 206 B.C., China was a united country under one ruler, Qin Shi Huangdi. He began the Qin dynasty, or ruling family.

Over the next 1,400 years, four other dynasties followed, and China grew into a great civilization. In 1206, the Mongol leader Genghis Khan became China's first non-Chinese emperor. The Mongols were followed by the Ming dynasty, and then the Qing. The Qing emperors were Manchus. As early as the 1500s ships from Portugal, Spain, and Britain came to China to trade. Britain later sold opium to China. But a Chinese ban on the drug led to the Opium War with Britain. In the war, China lost Hong Kong and other lands to the British.

In the late 19th and early 20th centuries, the Chinese rebelled against the Qing emperors and the Qing dynasty ended. In 1911, China became a republic. But the country was torn by fighting between rival warlords. Two opposing political movements grew up, the Communists and the Nationalists. These two groups fought the Japanese, who invaded Manchuria in 1931, and also fought each other. The Japanese left, and in 1949 the Communists, led by Mao Zedong, finally triumphed.

Under Communism, industry and farming came under state control. Recently, some of these controls have been eased. But power remains firmly in the hands of the Communist Party.

LANGUAGE

China's official language is *putonghua*, or Mandarin Chinese. This is similar to the Chinese spoken around Beijing. In Guangdong Province and Hong Kong, people speak in the Cantonese dialect.

Written Chinese is based on a picture language that is 4,000 years old. About 50,000 characters, or symbols, make up written Chinese. But only about 5,000 of them are used often. The modern way of writing Chinese words so that they can be read in English is called *pinyin*.

Useful words and phrases

English	*Chinese*
Zero	*líng*
One	*yí*
Two	*èr (liang)*
Three	*sān*
Four	*sì*
Five	*w*
Six	*lìu*
Seven	*qī*
Eight	*bā*
Nine	*ji*
Ten	*shí*
Sunday	*xīngqī tiān*
Monday	*xīngqī yí*
Tuesday	*xīngqī èr*

Useful words and phrases

English	*Chinese*
Wednesday	*xīngqī sān*
Thursday	*xīngqī sì*
Friday	*xīngqī w*
Saturday	*xīngqī lìu*
Good morning	*z o chén h o*
Hello, good day	*ní h o*
Good evening	*w n shàng h o*
Good night	*w n ān*
Good-bye	*zài jiàn*
Please	*q ng*
Thank you	*xìe xìe*
How are you?	*ní h o mā?*

INDEX

Note: Many familiar names for places in China have been replaced. For example: Mount Everest is Zhumulangma Feng; the Yangtze and Yellow rivers are now the Chang Jiang and Huang He, respectively.

Acknowledgments
Book created for Highlights for Children, Inc., by Bender Richardson White.
Editors: Peter MacDonald and Lionel Bender
Designer: Malcolm Smythe
Art Editor: Ben White
Editorial Assistant: Madeleine Samuel
Picture Researcher: Annabel Ossel
Production: Kim Richardson

Maps produced by Oxford Cartographers, England.
Banknotes from MRI Bankers Guide to Foreign Currency.
Stamps courtesy of Scott Publishing Co., Sidney, OH 45365 (www.scottonline.com).

Editorial Consultant: Andrew Gutelle.
Guide to China is approved by the China National Tourist Office, London.
Consultants: Bi Bingbin, Editor, External Service, Central China Television, Beijing; Hsin-Lin Wu, The Hsin Yi Foundation, Taiwan.
Managing Editor, Highlights New Products: Margie Hayes Richmond.

Picture credits
EU = Eye Ubiquitous, Z = Zefa. t = top, b = bottom, l = left, r = right. Cover: Brent T. Madison/MadisonImages. Pages: 6-7, 7b: EU/Julia Waterlow. 7t: Bjønar Johansen/DAS Photographs. 8: Luca Tettoni/Viesti Associates. 9t: EU/Julia Waterlow. 9b: Ken Ross/Viesti Associates. 10: Z/Damm. 11t: EU/Julia Waterlow. 11b: Z/Dr. P. Thiele. 12l: Katherine Feng. 13: EU/A. Carroll. 12r: Z/Dr. H. Kramarz. 14l: EU/A. Carroll. 14r: Z/Scholtz. 15: Sally and Richard Greenhill. 16l: EU/Julia Waterlow. 16-17: Z/K. Goebel. 17t: Bjønar Johansen/DAS Photographs. 18: Walter Bibikow. 19t: EU/Julia Waterlow. 19b: Z/Camerman. 20, 21t, 21b: EU/Julia Waterlow. 22: Z/E. Weiland. 23t: EU/Julia Waterlow. 23b: EU/L. Johnstone. 24l: Z. 24-25: Z/Sunak. 25r: EU/Julia Waterlow. 26, 27t, 27b: Sally and Richard Greenhill. 28, 29: Z/K. Goebel. 30: Z. Illustration on page 1 by Tom Powers.